WAITING

by Gail Young

ǁSAMUEL FRENCHǁ

FOR PRODUCTION ENQUIRIES

UNITED KINGDOM AND WORLD
EXCLUDING NORTH AMERICA
licensing@concordtheatricals.co.uk

020-7054-7298

NORTH AMERICA
info@concordtheatricals.com
1-866-979-0447

Each title is subject to availability from Concord Theatricals,
depending upon country of performance.

WAITING premiered in the Garret Theatre, Storyhouse, Chester, in November 2023. The production was directed by Yvette Owen, with set design by Ed Ringstead and Men in Sheds, costume design by Sarah Bell, Peter Russell and Gill James, lighting design by Mark Shenton and Alan Roberts, sound design by Andy Walker, digital imagery & films by Dan Cross and Chat Noir Productions, props by Charlotte Offley and publicity by Paul Crofts. The production stage manager was Vanessa Cuthbert. The cast was as follows:

PETER WRIGHT	Ally Goodman
JESSIE WRIGHT	Kat Tanczos
TOMMY WRIGHT	Ethan Harrison
JEAN WRIGHT	Savannah Bristow
SHIRLEY WRIGHT	Cara Sconce
AMY WRIGHT	Dawn Adams
DAVID WRIGHT	Dan Aynsley
TERESA DOHERTY	Felicity Parry
EDDIE GALLAGHER	Mike Howard
EILEEN GALLAGHER	Andrea Jones
CHURCH CHOIR & PUB SINGERS	Jen Baker, Julian Eyre, Gillian Eyre, Anna Morris, William Shaw
PUB MUSICIANS	Chris Elliott & Steve Lincoln
BBC RADIO ANNOUNCER (VOICE)	Julian Eyre
OWEN (VOICE)	Steffan Jorgensen
POSH TEA LADY (VOICE)	Sarah Bell
MATRON (VOICE)	Anna Morris

CHARACTERS

PETER WRIGHT – a Liverpool carter
JESSIE WRIGHT – his wife
TOMMY WRIGHT – their son and eldest child
JEAN WRIGHT – their eldest daughter
SHIRLEY WRIGHT – their youngest daughter
AMY WRIGHT (MAM) – mother to Peter and David
DAVID WRIGHT – Peter's younger brother
TERESA DOHERTY – David's sweetheart
EDDIE GALLAGHER – Teresa's uncle
EILEEN GALLAGHER – Teresa's aunty

CHURCH CHOIR & PUB SINGERS

BBC RADIO ANNOUNCER – Voice only
OWEN – Voice only
POSH WOMAN – Voice only
MATRON IN THE MATERNITY WARD – Voice only

SETTING

Bootle, Liverpool

TIME

May 1939 to May 1941

NOTES ON STAGING

I usually direct the premiere of my plays, but with *Waiting* I stepped into the role of producer, and handed the directorial reins to the very able and creative Yvette Owen.

We shared decisions over the imagery used in the show. This is a play that features many changes of location, and needs to easily move from one place to another to ensure that the pace and flow of the show does not suffer.

The decision was made to have a multi-functional static set that easily served a wide variety of purposes, and to use a mix of projected imagery and short films to take our audiences with us on the journey of the Wright family in this World War Two drama.

Historically accurate images and short films were projected onto a large sign for 'Tate & Lyle' - a well known factory in Liverpool at that time. Some scenes were filmed in black and white in a local church/cottage/ graveyard – namely the wedding scene, the funeral, and the children writing home from a cottage in Wales.

All of this added a great deal of depth, variety and authenticity to the premiere, and I would encourage directors and producers to give this aspect of their show a great deal of thought in the very early stages of their production as it will add so much to their interpretation of the script.

Check out the play-specific page on my website for more information and images at www.gailyoungplaywright.com, and the play-specific Facebook page.

Happy to share thoughts on imagery used in the premiere!

AUTHOR'S NOTE

I completed the first draft of *Waiting* years ago when on the Playwright Programme with the Liverpool Everyman and Playhouse. Since then I've revisited and edited the script countless times, but always put it aside to complete other writing projects and to stage other shows.

The truth is I was a bit of a coward about finishing the whole thing. There's no escaping the fact that war is a tough and scary thing to write about. It's a real struggle to believe that you've done both the subject and the characters justice on the page and on the stage.

But in the end the story of my mum's family in Liverpool in World War Two kept calling me back to *Waiting*, and this play is very loosely based on their experiences and what happened to the city during that time. I hope I've managed to capture the love, humour and stoicism that pulled the Wright family and the wider community through a terrible chapter in Liverpool's history.

Producing and writing the play has been a really personal journey for me, and I can't thank the director, cast and crew enough for finally bringing my script to life.

It was worth the wait.

Gail Young
2025

ACT ONE

Scene One – May 1939

(The image of a 1930s radio dominates the stage. It crackles into life.)

RADIO ANNOUNCER. Germany and Italy have today signed a new formal alliance – the 'Pact of Steel' – confirming that they will be fully committed allies in the event of war. In light of this announcement, the Prime Minister is currently holding urgent talks with the Cabinet to review the policy of appeasement and our country's next steps.

> *(The image and broadcast fade as lights come up on* **JESSIE WRIGHT** *and her three children in their sparsely furnished but clean and tidy home in a working-class terraced house in Bootle, Liverpool.* **JESSIE** *and her daughters* **JEAN** *and* **SHIRLEY** *are busy making long paper flower garlands.)*

> *(***TOMMY*** is totally bored, and gives a huge sigh.)*

JESSIE. What's up with you?

TOMMY. *(Indicating the flowers.)* THESE! Flipping flowers...

JEAN. Stop moaning will yer Tommy.

SHIRLEY. Yeah – stop yer moaning will yer.

TOMMY. Button it you two.

JESSIE. We're doing this for Prince remember – for the May Horse Parade.

TOMMY. Why can't I just go up to the stables with me dad and groom Prince instead? This... *(Holds up the flowers.)* This...is...women's work!

> *(JESSIE laughs.)*

JESSIE. Listen to you...'Women's work.'

TOMMY. It is! I'm not a little lad anymore.

JEAN & SHIRLEY. Ooooh. 'I'm not a little lad any more.'

TOMMY. Shut up will yer.

JEAN & SHIRLEY. 'Shut up will yer.'

JESSIE. Leave him alone girls.

SHIRLEY. I hope Prince wins 'Best in Show' again Mam.

JEAN. Look...I've finished another one!

> *(JEAN holds up her finished garland. SHIRLEY grabs it and places it round her neck. She dances around the room as PETER WRIGHT enters unseen, and observes his family. JEAN spots him.)*

Dad!

> *(The girls rush to PETER.)*

SHIRLEY. Do you like me necklace Dad?

PETER. It's beautiful Shirley.

SHIRLEY. Our Jean made it.

PETER. Did you Queen?

JEAN. And I made them as well.

(She points to a pile of finished garlands on the table.)

SHIRLEY. And me!

PETER. You've been a right pair of busy bees haven't you? So – as a thank you...

*(He produces three oranges from his pockets and juggles with them. He chucks one each to **JEAN** and **SHIRLEY**, and tosses one over to **TOMMY**.)*

JESSIE. Where did you get those?

PETER. Fell off the back of a cart.

JESSIE. You wanna be careful. The amount you're lifting down at the docks – they'll think you're starting a fruit and veg stall.

*(**JEAN** helps **PETER** take off his jacket and he hands her his cap.)*

PETER. Thanks love.

SHIRLEY. Where's Prince?

PETER. Outside. The old lad's pulled that cart all over town today. Shifted a lot of heavy loads up from the docks.

*(He looks over at a scowling **TOMMY**.)*

What's up with you?

TOMMY. Nothing...

PETER. Oh aye?

*(**TOMMY** chucks his paper flowers down.)*

TOMMY. I've felt like a right girl's blouse making these.

PETER. Alright. Alright. Keep your hair on.

TOMMY. I'm not making them flowers anymore Dad… I'm not!… I'm…I'm a man – not a girl!

(**PETER** *considers* **TOMMY***'s declaration.*)

PETER. Suppose he's got a point.

JESSIE. He's eleven! And he's hardly made any!

PETER. Only a couple of more years left at school so…

(*Pause.*)

No more making flower garlands for you son.

TOMMY. Yesssss!!!!

PETER. You can come up to the yard with me now if you like eh? Help me make a start on getting Prince's coat gleaming for the parade.

(*There is a sudden loud whinnying from the hallway.*)

JESSIE. Is that front door open?

(*Another whinny.*)

Not again Peter!

(**JESSIE** *runs from the room.* **JEAN, SHIRLEY** *and* **TOMMY** *giggle.*)

(*Offstage.*) Out – get out Prince! Get those muddy hooves off my front step. I've just cleaned that today! Go on – get out will you.

(*We hear the front door slam.* **JESSIE** *enters.*)

That's the second time this week Peter! Shut that flaming door in future!

PETER. Calm down will yer. He's part of the family isn't he?

JESSIE. I don't want to see his big head looming in that hallway again!

(JEAN and SHIRLEY giggle.)

Right you two – time for bed. You can keep those oranges for tomorrow. Give 'em here.

PETER. Give your old dad a kiss.

(JEAN and SHIRLEY kiss PETER.)

JESSIE. And don't be too long up at that stable yard Peter. Your tea'll be ready soon.

PETER. What are you dishing up?

SHIRLEY. We've had ours.

TOMMY. It's Friday Dad!

PETER. No...don't tell me...

JEAN. Go on Dad – have a guess.

PETER. Wait...wait...it's coming to me.

TOMMY, JEAN & SHIRLEY. Fish!!!!

*(Lights fade on the Wright home and come up on the tack room at the stable. **PETER** is performing his nightly ritual of cleaning/ polishing Prince's halter and reins. We hear the sound of horses settling down for the night. **TOMMY** enters. He's carrying the dandy brush and comb for Prince's mane, and puts the kit away in an old storage box.)*

PETER. All done?

TOMMY. Yep

PETER. He wouldn't harm a fly. But you still need to be careful around him – do you hear? He's a big old stallion remember...

TOMMY. I know.

(**PETER** *finishes cleaning the bridle as*
TOMMY *tidies things away.*)

PETER. Time we were getting home. You've got school
tomorrow.

TOMMY. I hate school.

PETER. No you don't.

TOMMY. I do! It's frigging boring. I wanna work here
with you.

PETER. Less of that bloody swearing.

TOMMY. You swear.

PETER. That's different.

(**TOMMY** *hangs up the cleaned tack.*)

TOMMY. Dad.

PETER. Yeah?

TOMMY. In school today Billy Williams was saying that
there's gonna be another war soon. You know – like the
Great War.

PETER. Oh aye.

TOMMY. Me Grandad fought in that war didn't he?

PETER. He did.

TOMMY. Was he a hero Dad?

PETER. They all were son.

TOMMY. I wish I could have met him.

PETER. So do I.

TOMMY. Will you fight Dad – if there is another war – will
yer? Like Grandad did?

PETER. That Billy Williams has filled your head full of
nonsense.

TOMMY. Well – if there is a war – I wanna be a pilot!

> (**TOMMY** *careers around, acting like an aeroplane and enthusiastically shooting down the enemy.* **PETER** *uneasily watches on as the lights fade on the scene, and* **TOMMY***'s childish sound effects change to the real sound of enemy air fire.*)
>
> (*Blackout.*)

Scene Two – May 1939

(1939. The May Parade. Liverpool Waterfront. An image of a garlanded shire horse dominates the stage. It is a fairground atmosphere with stalls and games, and the 'Best in Show' competition for the horses is just finishing. **JESSIE** *watches* **JEAN** *and* **SHIRLEY** *play on a hoopla stall.* **TOMMY** *is kicking a football around.)*

JESSIE. *(Shouting.)* Tommy! Get over here.

*(***TOMMY*** does as he's told.)*

Give me your jacket. I don't want that covered in muck.

*(***TOMMY*** hands **JESSIE** the jacket. He spots one of his mates in the distance, and boots the ball offstage, shouting as he does so.)*

TOMMY. There's the lads... HEY... BILLY! BILLY...

*(***TOMMY*** rushes off. **JESSIE** shouts after him.)*

JESSIE. Be careful with that ball you! Do you hear me?

*(***JESSIE*** rejoins the girls at the stall. **DAVID WRIGHT**, Peter's younger brother, enters with his latest girlfriend – **TERESA DOHERTY**. He tiptoes up to **JESSIE** and taps her on the shoulder. She spins around.)*

David!

*(***JEAN*** and **SHIRLEY** scream in delight at seeing their uncle. He swings them both around until they are giddy and giggly.)*

DAVID. Look at you two – I think you've grown again!

JEAN. I'm a lot taller than our Shirley.

SHIRLEY. Not that much! Look.

> (*She stands back-to-back with* **JEAN.** **DAVID** *measures them up against each other.*)

DAVID. Well... Jean's taller – but there's not a lot in it.

> (*He takes some money from his pocket and hands it to them.*)

Here you go girls. Go and treat yourselves to some candy floss.

JEAN & SHIRLEY. Thanks Uncle Dave.

> (*They skip off.* **JESSIE** *tuts.*)

JESSIE. That was too much money David.

DAVID. Oh leave off will you Jessie. Let 'em have bit of fun will yer.

> (**JESSIE** *looks* **TERESA** *up and down. Her old dress can't compete with* **TERESA**'s *new outfit.*)

Oh – where's me manners eh? Teresa – this is my sister-in-law Jessie.

TERESA. Nice to meet you Jessie.

> (*A forced smile from* **JESSIE**.)

DAVID. Where's our Peter?

JESSIE. Over there (*She points offstage.*) near the parade ring with Prince.

DAVID. Oh aye... Peter – PETER!

> (*He charges off.*)
>
> (*Awkward pause.*)
>
> (**JESSIE** *breaks the silence.*)

JESSIE. Have you known David long?

TERESA. A while. I met him through me Aunty Eileen. You might know her. David says she lives not that far from you.

JESSIE. Eileen?

TERESA. Eileen and Eddie?

JESSIE. Eileen and Eddie? Can't say I do... I'll have to get me thinking cap on...

TERESA. I've been living with them for a few months now – since I moved over from Newry... Eileen is my mum's sister... They haven't got any children of their own, and they've treated me like a daughter... they're very kind...

>   *(Another silence.)*

It's good to have a day off work isn't it? I love the weekends!

JESSIE. Where do you work?

TERESA. With Eileen in the post office in town. She put a good word in for me – you know – about my exam results and that – and they took me on. It's working out just fine.

>   *(**JESSIE** nods in acknowledgement.)*

How about you Jessie?

JESSIE. Sorry?

TERESA. Do you work?

JESSIE. Oh...cleaning...you know...different places.

TERESA. Oh yes?

JESSIE. Every little helps doesn't it?

TERESA. You're right there.

*(**PETER** and **DAVID** enter.)*

JESSIE. Did Prince win?

PETER. No rosettes this year. Bit of an old soldier now isn't he.

DAVID. You did a great job with those flower garlands Jessie. But that young grey stallion over there won first prize. *(He points offstage.)*

> *(**JESSIE** and **DAVID** look over at the winner. **PETER** and **TERESA** nod hello to each other while the other two are engrossed in the horse parade.)*

PETER. *(Indicating himself.)* Peter.

TERESA. *(Indicating herself.)* Teresa.

> *(**JESSIE** spots her daughters.)*

JESSIE. Will you look at the state of those two!

> *(**JEAN** and **SHIRLEY** enter carrying enormous candy floss sticks, some of which is stuck in their long hair.)*

How have you managed to get that stuck in your hair? Come here will you.

> *(**JESSIE** and **TERESA** busy themselves sorting the girls' hair out.)*

DAVID. It's a good parade again.

PETER. Not bad.

DAVID. Yeah.

PETER. Not seen you for a while – what's new with you?

DAVID. Oh, this and that... you know... this and that...

> *(A silent beat as **PETER** looks to his younger brother for more information.)*

PETER. This and that? I've not seen you for weeks and that's the best you can come up with? Waddya mean 'This and that'?

(**DAVID** *pulls* **PETER** *to one side.*)

DAVID. I'm joining the navy.

PETER. *(Laughs.)* The navy?

DAVID. The Royal Navy. I've decided…

PETER. *(Interrupting.)* What do you wanna go and do that for?

DAVID. The way things are going…in the news…you know… After what happened to our dad, I wanna be there on the front line if anything kicks off – when the time comes…fight for me country. Don't you ever think about it?

PETER. Listen David – don't go rushing into anything…

(*He is interrupted by* **JESSIE.**)

JESSIE. *(Loudly.)* Oh for God's sake – stand still will you Shirley! There. *(The hair is finally disentangled.)* That's better.

JEAN. Can we have a go on the coconut shy Mam?

(**SHIRLEY** *grabs* **TERESA**'s *hand.*)

SHIRLEY. Come with us. You can have a go too.

TERESA. *(To* **JESSIE.**) Shall we?

JEAN. Come on Mum.

JESSIE. Alright. I'm coming, I'm coming!

(**JEAN** *and* **SHIRLEY** *drag* **JESSIE** *and* **TERESA** *offstage.* **DAVID** *and* **PETER** *watch them go.*)

DAVID. What do you think of her then?

PETER. Who?

DAVID. Who? Teresa of course!

PETER. I...er...I've only just met her.

DAVID. She's a stunner isn't she? I don't mind telling you I'm smitten...

(**PETER** *stares after* **TERESA**.)

PETER. How long have you known her?

DAVID. Couple of months.

PETER. You've kept that quiet.

DAVID. I really wanted you to meet her today because...

(**DAVID** *can't finish the sentence. Pause.*)

PETER. And what Casanova? ...And what?

(*No reply.*)

Are you trying to tell me that you're serious about this one...about you and her?

DAVID. Yeah...s'pose... I'm...I'm thinking of asking her to... you know... (*He mumbles.*) marry me.

PETER. Sorry?

DAVID. (*Louder.*) To marry me.

(*Pause.*)

So – waddya think?

PETER. What do I think? You haven't known her that long... I dunno Dave...you're a long time married remember.

DAVID. I'm not asking you for permission! I'll count meself lucky if she says 'Yes'.

(*Pause.*)

DAVID. Just don't tell anyone else will yer.

PETER. Have you told me mam?

DAVID. No...not yet

PETER. Good luck with that.

DAVID. Meaning?

PETER. Meaning you know what she's like.

> (**JEAN, SHIRLEY, JESSIE** *and* **TERESA** *enter.*
> **SHIRLEY** *proudly carries a coconut.*)

SHIRLEY. Look what I've won Dad.

PETER. Well done Queen.

> (**DAVID** *realises the time.*)

DAVID. Hey...come on Teresa. We've gotta dash. Sorry to love you and leave you folks, but we're off to the pictures.

> (**DAVID** *hugs* **SHIRLEY** *and* **JEAN** *goodbye.*)

TERESA. Oh yes. *Gone with the Wind.* Have you seen it yet Jessie?

JESSIE. No. Lucky you.

TERESA. We're off to the early showing – I can't wait. Bye girls.

JEAN & SHIRLEY. Bye.

> (**JESSIE** *and* **PETER** *watch them hurry away.*)

JESSIE. Pretty girl.

PETER. S'pose so.

JESSIE. He doesn't introduce us to all of them.

PETER. True.

JESSIE. She's Eileen and Eddie's niece.

PETER. Is she now... Who's Eileen and Eddie?

JESSIE. They go to the singalong in the pub on Friday nights.

PETER. Do they? *(He still looks blank.)*

JESSIE. It took me a while to think who they were – you do know him – he thinks he's Bootle's answer to Bing Crosby.

PETER. Oh him! Well I hope she can hold a tune better than he can.

JESSIE. Did you know that they're...

PETER. Left footers.

JESSIE. Yes – I s'pose she's a Catholic...

> *(**PETER** interrupts as he spots his mother in the distance.)*

PETER. Hey up. Here's me mam – with our Tommy in tow.

JESSIE. What's he been up to now!

> *(**JEAN** and **SHIRLEY** shout and wave over to their nan.)*

JEAN & SHIRLEY. Over here Nan! We're over here!

> *(**MAM** enters holding **TOMMY** by the scruff of the neck. **TOMMY** clutches his football. She thrusts him into **PETER**'s arms.)*

MAM. This one needs a firmer hand Peter. He kicked that football right into the stalls. Absolute bedlam!

> *(**MAM** turns to **JEAN** and **SHIRLEY**.)*

My – don't you two look pretty! Give us a twirl.

> *(**JEAN** and **SHIRLEY** oblige.)*

Lovely! *(To **JESSIE**.)* Is that a new hat?

JESSIE. No.

MAM. It goes well with your dress.

JESSIE. It should do. They're both ancient.

> *(The sound of distant thunder as the sky begins to darken. **SHIRLEY** runs to **JESSIE**.)*

MAM. Bless her. She's frightened of the thunder.

JESSIE. Who she gets that from God only knows.

MAM. Not me.

PETER. You're right there – it'd take a lot to scare you.

MAM. Less of the cheek you. *(She looks around.)* Didn't I see our David over here before? Wasn't he with someone?

> *(A bolt of lightning flashes across the semi-darkened stage. A massive clap of thunder.)*

> *(They all look up as one. The rumbling thunder now resembles the sound of approaching bombers.)*

> *(Blackout.)*

Scene Three – May 1939

(The cinema. **DAVID** *and* **TERESA** *watch the end of* Gone With The Wind.* *Tears roll down* **TERESA***'s cheeks.)*

TERESA. I'm sorry.

DAVID. For what?

TERESA. Crying! Wasn't it emotional though?

*(***DAVID*** tries to look suitably moved.)*

DAVID. Emotional? Er...yeah... Oh yeah...very! Very emotional.

TERESA. Vivien Leigh...she's so so beautiful. And Clark Gable...

DAVID. Yeah...yeah... Mind you he wasn't very nice to her when he left her was he? *(He mimics Clark Gable.)* "Frankly my dear I don't give a damn."

*(***TERESA*** laughs and then checks her watch.)*

TERESA. Let's get a move on. I don't want to miss the tram.

*(***DAVID*** does a quick reccy of the cinema.)*

DAVID. Hang on a minute Teresa...hang on...before we go...

(He goes down on one knee.)

TERESA. David! What are you doing?

---

* A licence to produce *Waiting* does not include the right to publicly exhibit the film *Gone With The Wind*. The publisher and author suggest that the licensee contact Warner Bros. Discovery or its designee, to licence or acquire permission for exhibition of the film. If a licence or permission is unattainable for *Gone With The Wind*, the licensee must ensure that the film cannot be seen or heard during the production.

DAVID. Frankly my dear, I DO give a damn! So – marry me Teresa?

> *(Pause.)*

TERESA. I don't know what to say David, its such a...

DAVID. *(Interrupting.)* I know it's all a bit sudden like, but...I love you...I really do.

> *(She gently shushes him.)*

TERESA. Yes...yes... I will marry you.

DAVID. I haven't bought the ring yet...no time...

> *(She silences him with a kiss.)*

> *('God Save The King' suddenly blares out.*)*

Sod that. Come on – you've got that tram to catch!

> *(They rush out as the national anthem continues.)*

> *(Blackout.)*

---

* A licence to produce *Waiting* does not include a performance licence for any third-party or copyrighted recordings. Licensees should create their own.

Scene Four – August 1939

(The image of the front page of a newspaper dated 28th August 1939 dominates the stage. The headline reads 'GERMANY ALIGNS ON POLISH BORDER'.*)

(As the image fades, lights come up on Jessie and Peter's home. It is late evening. **PETER** *is engrossed in a newspaper with the same headline.* **JESSIE** *knits a child's jumper.)*

JESSIE. You've always got your head stuck in that newspaper.

PETER. Hmmm??

JESSIE. I said – you've always got your head stuck in that newspaper.

*(***PETER** *doesn't look up.)*

PETER. Yeah, well...there's a lot going on in the world.

(They continue knitting and reading.)

JESSIE. Do you think we will go to war?

PETER. Hmmmmm?

JESSIE. *(Louder.)* I said, do you think we will go to war?

*(***PETER** *continues to read.)*

Well – if we do – I don't want you doing anything stupid, do you hear me?

PETER. Stop your worrying will you? Nothing's happened yet.

---

* A licence to produce *Waiting* does not include a licence to publicly display any third-party or copyrighted images. Licensees must acquire rights for any copyrighted images or create their own.

JESSIE. But it will...I know it will...

PETER. How do you know?

JESSIE. I've heard them...on the radio...and I've watched you reading that bloody newspaper every night like your life depends on it...and then there's your David.

PETER. What about David?

JESSIE. Joining the Royal Navy. Your mam's not happy about it! Why's he gone and done that?

PETER. He fancied a change I s'pose.

JESSIE. Don't lie to me Peter. I've heard you two talking. It's coz he wants to be like your dad – 'serve his country' and all that rubbish.

PETER. It's not rubbish.

JESSIE. Well it is to me. I don't want my husband buggering off to war – I don't.

(**PETER** *finally lowers the paper.*)

PETER. What are you going on about?

JESSIE. You know what I'm going on about. I don't want you doing what your dad did, leaving your mam with two lads to rear on her own. I'm not having it Peter – do you hear me? I'm not having it.

(*No reply from* **PETER**. **JESSIE** *tidies away her knitting.*)

Anyway – I'm tired. Think I'll have an early night. You coming?

PETER. In a minute.

(*She ruffles* **PETER**'s *hair as she leaves.* **PETER** *reads the front page of the newspaper as the headline slowly dominates the stage again. He exits, turning the light off as he goes.*)

(Momentary darkness.)

(The image of the radio fills the stage. It crackles into life.)

(Neville Chamberlain announces that Britain is at war with Germany.)

(The date is third of September 1939.)

(The image slowly fades.)

(Blackout.)

Scene Five – Mid September 1939

(Peter and Jessie's home is littered with the children's belongings – gas masks and boxes, small packed bags, children's coats, Tommy's football boots and his football, and Jean's book – Black Beauty *by Anna Sewell.)*

*(**JESSIE** enters hugging Shirley's doll Victoria. She surveys the scene.)*

*(**MAM** bustles in carrying three brown paper bags containing ham butties, three apples, and a large bottle of water for the journey.)*

MAM. Just a few butties for them and an apple for the journey. It's not a lot – but it's good ham. I cooked it meself... And the bread's nice and fresh. I'll give the water to our Jean to carry on the train. Tommy can't be trusted with it. He'd forget his head if it wasn't screwed on...

(She is stopped in her tracks by the sight of the gas masks and the name tags. She picks up a name tag.)

Like little parcels...

(Pause.)

JESSIE. I don't want them to go.

MAM. But they've got to go love.

JESSIE. Billy Williams and his little sister aren't going. I've told Peter but he won't listen.

MAM. He wants them safe.

JESSIE. So do I!

MAM. But the government have said...

JESSIE. *(Interrupting.)* The government! The government! If I hear one more word about the flaming government.

(**PETER** *rushes in.*)

PETER. They've not gone yet?

MAM. Thank God you've made it. Work let you off then?

PETER. Work don't know.

(**JESSIE** *is pacing the floor.*)

JESSIE. They're not going Peter.

PETER. They've got to – to be safe love.

(**TOMMY** *bursts into the room, very excited.*)

TOMMY. It's here! The bus to the train station is here!

(**SHIRLEY** *dances in.* **JEAN** *quietly follows her.*)

SHIRLEY. Nana! It's here! It's here. We're going on our holidays!

MAM. Yes Queen. I know.

(**SHIRLEY** *picks up her doll.*)

SHIRLEY. And Victoria is coming with me as well.

MAM. Is she?

(**SHIRLEY** *nods enthusiastically.*)

SHIRLEY. I've never been to Wales. Will it be nice Nana?

MAM. It'll be lovely Shirley. Really lovely.

TOMMY. There's fields everywhere you know. Loads of places to play football.

SHIRLEY. And sheep. Lots and lots of sheep!

(**SHIRLEY** *grabs her coat,* **JESSIE** *helps her put it on.* **TOMMY** *hurls on his jacket, and grabs*

his gas mask and football boots/ball. His nan
pulls him back to tie his name tag onto his coat.)

MAM. Wait Tommy! You have to wear this name tag.

(**TOMMY** *and* **MAM** *bustle out of the room.*
PETER *goes to pick up Shirley's name tag but*
JESSIE *snatches it from him. She kneels to tie*
it on her youngest child's coat.)

SHIRLEY. *(Reading her name tag.)* Shirley Wright. That's me!

JESSIE. *(Hugging* **SHIRLEY** *tight.)* That's you love. Shirley
Wright. And don't you ever ever forget it...

(**JESSIE** *exits with* **SHIRLEY** *and her*
belongings, shouting to **JEAN** *as she goes.)*

Jean? Come on love – hurry up!

(**JEAN** *slowly pulls on her coat.* **PETER** *looks*
at her book.)

PETER. *Black Beauty* eh? You must have read that book a
hundred times. Just think – you'll see loads of horses
in Wales.

JEAN. They won't be like our Prince... I don't wanna go
Dad...

(**PETER** *sits on a chair and draws* **JEAN** *onto*
his knee. They sit in momentary sad silence.)

PETER. I need you to go – to look after Shirley and Tommy.

JEAN. Tommy's the oldest.

PETER. But you're the wisest.

(Another sad silence as **JEAN** *hands* **PETER**
the name tag which he ties onto her coat.
They hug.)

Just remember that we'll be here waiting for you to come home. And you will, you know Jean – you will come back – all of you – very very soon. And we'll all still be here – waiting for you.

(**TOMMY** *rushes in.*)

TOMMY. Gerra frigging move on Jean! The bus is here.

PETER. What have I told you about bloody swearing!

TOMMY. Sorry Dad – but COME ON WILL YER!!

(**TOMMY** *charges out as* **JESSIE** *rushes in.*)

JESSIE. Come on Jean – hurry up love.

(**JESSIE** *grabs* **JEAN**'s *belongings and hurries her out of the room, giving* **PETER** *a parting shot as she does so.*)

If anything happens to them Peter – ANYTHING...

(*Lights fade on* **PETER** *alone onstage.*)

(*Blackout.*)

Scene Six – January 1940

(A huge portrait image of a World War One soldier haunts the stage.* It is Jim Wright, Mam's dead husband and David and Peter's father.)

(As the image slowly fades, lights come up on Mam's home. The table is laden with her best china. A home-cooked Victoria sponge dominates the display. A framed image of Jim is in the room.)

*(**DAVID** is wearing his dark blue Royal Navy uniform. He is seated at the table with **TERESA** and **MAM** who are both in their Sunday best. There is an oppressive silence. **MAM** pours **TERESA** a cup of tea.)*

MAM. Sugar?

TERESA. Yes please.

*(**MAM** passes **TERESA** the sugar bowl.)*

Thank you.

*(**TERESA** has one teaspoon of sugar and passes the sugar bowl to **DAVID**. **TERESA** stirs her tea. Her spoon rattles against the cup.)*

(Quietly.) Could I just have a bit more milk please David?

*(**DAVID** passes the milk jug to her. She adds a generous amount of milk to her tea, stirring the cup as quietly as she can.)*

---

* A licence to produce *Waiting* does not include a licence to publicly display any third-party or copyrighted images. Licensees must acquire rights for any copyrighted images or create their own.

(Pause.)

DAVID. Mam doesn't like her tea too milky – do you Mam?

MAM. No.

(Silence as they all sip their tea.)

The Royal Navy are getting their money's worth out of you aren't they son? How many more trips are they going to send you on?

TERESA. He looks good in the uniform though doesn't he Mrs Wright?

*(**MAM** glares at **TERESA**.)*

MAM. He looks good in anything. He didn't need to join the Royal Navy to impress me.

DAVID. Look Mam, I joined up because...

MAM. *(Interrupting.)* Without talking to me first! That's what you did. After what happened to your father and all.

DAVID. Well there's no going back now.

(Silence again as they sip their tea. Eventually...)

Any chance of a slice of that cake Mam?

MAM. Of course. It's your favourite. Victoria sponge.

*(**MAM** cuts **DAVID** a very generous slice and hands the plate to him.)*

Teresa?

TERESA. Oh yes please.

*(**MAM** cuts **TERESA** a miserly slice of cake and hands the plate to her.)*

*(**DAVID** tucks into his Victoria sponge.)*

DAVID. I've missed this.

MAM. Nothing like a bit of home cooking is there son?

DAVID. Nope.

MAM. Do you bake Teresa?

TERESA. Oh no...no... I'm not a very good cook I'm afraid.

MAM. No?

TERESA. No.

MAM. Oh.

> *(Pause.)*

DAVID. But she's learning aren't you?

> *(**TERESA** nods. **MAM** is stony-faced.)*

Her Aunty Eileen has promised to teach her how to cook a good Sunday dinner before we get married.

MAM. That's nice.

> *(**DAVID** holds out his empty plate. **MAM** cuts him another enormous slice.)*

DAVID. That's what we wanted to talk about today.

TERESA. The wedding. We've seen the priest and...we're probably going to have it at Saint Alexander's...

> *(**MAM** glares at **DAVID**.)*

DAVID. *(Soldiering on.)* But we'll have to plan it round my leave...

TERESA. So we thought we might bring it forward with things being how they are... you know... the war...and things...

*(As she says this **TERESA** fiddles nervously with the crucifix on her necklace. **MAM** stares at the religious symbol.)*

MAM. I see.

(Silence again as they sip their tea.)

DAVID. Eddie and Eileen have asked me and you round to tea at theirs next Saturday Mam.

TERESA. They're really looking forward to it Mrs Wright.

*(**MAM** checks if the pot needs more water.)*

DAVID. Mam?

MAM. I'll just get some more hot water for the pot.

*(**MAM** exits with the teapot. **DAVID** wipes beads of sweat from his brow.)*

DAVID. Christ – this is hard going!

TERESA. Mmmm.

DAVID. Thanks for being here with me to talk to her about the wedding.

TERESA. I still think you need to give her a bit more time to think about it all.

DAVID. Why does she need more time? What's there to think about?

*(**MAM** overhears his remark as she re-enters the room carrying the pot.)*

MAM. A lot – there's a lot to think about. It's not every day that my son tells me he's getting married in a Catholic Church.

TERESA. Look Mrs Wright...

(**MAM** *plonks the refilled teapot down on the table.*)

MAM. No – you look young lady! I've already lost him to the Royal Navy while there's a war going on – and now you're telling me I'll be losing him to your religion! That's quite enough for one day.

DAVID. Mam!

TERESA. I'm sorry that you feel like that Mrs Wright.

(**TERESA** *snatches up her coat and handbag.*)

Goodbye. And thanks for the tea.

(*She pauses at the door.*)

Are you coming David?

(*He doesn't respond.* **TERESA** *sweeps out of the room.* **DAVID** *stands dithering.*)

(*Quick fade on Mam's house. Lights up on a street corner.*)

(**PETER** *bumps into a tearful* **TERESA** *running down the road.*)

PETER. Steady on.

TERESA. Sorry...sorry...

PETER. Teresa?

TERESA. Oh. It's you...

PETER. Are you alright?

(**TERESA** *bursts into tears.* **PETER** *puts his arm around her to comfort her.*)

Hey, hey. Don't cry.

(*She's embarrassed and turns away from him.*)

TERESA. Sorry.

PETER. What for?

TERESA. Sorry...

PETER. Stop apologising will you.

TERESA. Sorry...sorry... I said sorry again...

PETER. Who's upset you?

(*No answer.*)

Let me guess. Me mother?

(**TERESA** *nods.*)

I'm on my way there now.

TERESA. That'll be fun for you. She's a right bundle of laughs.

(**PETER** *smiles.*)

PETER. She's a hard woman alright. I hope he's worth the fight... Do you...

TERESA. (*Interrupting.*) Love him?

PETER. Do you? Because at the end of the day that's all that really matters.

(*The conversation is cut short by the sound of* **DAVID** *running towards them. He enters – out of breath and anxious.*)

DAVID. Teresa!

PETER. Someone's upset her.

DAVID. And we all know who!

PETER. I'm on me way there now.

DAVID. Well, have a word with her will you Peter – for our sake.

*(****DAVID*** *puts a protective arm around* ****TERESA.****)*

DAVID. Come on love. Let's get you home. See you Peter.

PETER. See you.

(Unseen by ****DAVID****, ****TERESA*** *and* ****PETER*** *exchange a long glance as the couple walk away, and* ****TERESA*** *mouths 'Thank You' to* ****PETER.****)*

(Lights cross fade to Mam's house.)

Scene Seven – January 1949

(Mam's house minutes later.)

MAM. That stupid boy! Your father will turn in his grave.

PETER. He's not a boy – he's a grown man.

MAM. Is she pregnant? Is she?

PETER. No! I mean... I don't think so...

MAM. Mind you, what would you know? Jessie trapped you good and proper didn't she! Little orphan Annie might have fooled you all those years ago, but she didn't fool me...

*(**PETER** gives his **MAM** a warning look.)*

PETER. Jessie doesn't deserve that.

(Pause.)

MAM. All the girls he's been out with – and he goes and picks her!

*(**MAM** reels off **DAVID**'s past conquests.)*

Louise Evans – now she was a pretty girl...a bit dim mind you...a penny for her thoughts would have been pricey! ...And what about Susan Edwards? He went out with her for ages. I really thought that she might be the one.

PETER. Mmmm.

MAM. I could have put up with that awful laugh – and at least she wasn't a Catholic!

*(**PETER** shoots his **MAM** a disapproving look.)*

Ruth Hardy – remember her? Her father had that corner shop. Not the best dresser I'll admit – and she needed to lose a bit of weight. But at least he'd have married into a bit of money with her!

(*Mournful pause.*)

Have you met her?

PETER. Ruth Hardy?

MAM. No soft lad! His latest conquest. Have you met her?

PETER. Yes.

MAM. When?

PETER. When? ...I er...I met her at the Horse Parade.

MAM. In May? Oh! So she's had plenty of time to get her claws into him then!

PETER. She seems...nice...a nice girl.

MAM. How do you know? You've only met her the once.

(*Pause.*)

She'll make him change his religion.

PETER. Stop that.

MAM. She will. She will. They all do! I'll have Catholic grandchildren. Left footers!

PETER. What's the difference as long as they're raised right?

MAM. That's typical of you isn't it? If it wasn't for Jessie your kids wouldn't ever see the inside of a church.

PETER. Don't start.

MAM. One of my son's a heathen and the other's going to be a Catholic. It's just not natural!

PETER. I don't know what you expect from him.

MAM. He deserves better.

PETER. Better? Bloody hell Mam, anyone would think he's a big catch the way you're carrying on. I don't remember you getting this hot and bothered about who I walked out with.

MAM. That was different.

PETER. What's that supposed to mean?

MAM. You were...

PETER. I was what?

MAM. You were the man of the house weren't you...after your dad died. You had a bit more about you. Well – I thought you did until you got Jessie in the family way!

PETER. The man of the house? I was a young lad Mam.

MAM. I know...but you grew up fast.

PETER. Too bloody fast. You couldn't get me out to work quick enough.

MAM. We did what we had to do to keep food on the table. And David was the...

PETER. *(Interrupting.)* The baby. I know. David was the baby...

(Pause.)

You've got to let him go sometime.

MAM. I know... cake?

(**PETER** *nods and she cuts him a slice. Momentary peace. Suddenly...)*

And why has he gone and joined the bloody Royal Navy? Why?

PETER. Me dad would have been proud of him – I know that.

MAM. Well I'm not! I don't want another telegram telling me another one of my family has gone and... *(She can't bring herself to say the word.)* I don't want that again... all for what eh? All for what...

*(Sad pause. Then **MAM** explodes.)*

And just to top it all off he's marrying a flaming Catholic!

PETER. *(Interrupting.)* Mam! That'll do.

(He puts on his cap.)

You love him remember. And he loves you. So think on.

(He kisses her and exits.)

*(**MAM** holds up the remaining Victoria sponge.)*

MAM. Victoria sponge... his favourite... I made him his favourite...

(She sadly clears the table as the lights fade on the scene.)

(Blackout.)

Scene Eight – March 1940

(The image of the front page of a newspaper dominates the stage. The headline reads 'HITLER DRAFTS JEWS FOR WORK'.*)

(As it fades, lights come up on the Wright household. **PETER** *is reading the paper with the same headline.* **JESSIE** *enters.)*

JESSIE. I've had Evie Bamford round here today – on the warpath again.

(No reply.)

You still haven't paid her for that window our Tommy smashed.

(Still no reply.)

It's ages ago now. And she wants paying. Kicked his football straight through their window he did – right into their front room.

PETER. Well he picked the right house.

JESSIE. Pardon?

PETER. It's full of bloody Evertonians.

JESSIE. God knows what he's up to in Wales. Probably turning into a proper little hooligan without us there to keep an eye on him.

PETER. Jessie – I'm not in the mood for your nagging tonight...

JESSIE. *(Interrupting.)* Not in the mood? Well Evie Bamford was in a right flaming mood and...

---

* A licence to produce *Waiting* does not include a licence to publicly display any third-party or copyrighted images. Licensees must acquire rights for any copyrighted images or create their own.

PETER. *(Interrupting.)* Give it a rest will you.

JESSIE. You've never backed me up with him, never! Too soft by half.

PETER. That's enough.

JESSIE. If I hear that he's up to any shenanigans in Wales...

>   (**PETER** *thumps his hand on the table.*)

PETER. I SAID THAT'S ENOUGH!

JESSIE. Alright! Alright! What the hell's up with you?

>   (*He stands, turning his back on her. He eventually breaks the silence.*)

PETER. I went to join up today.

JEAN. What? You...sorry...you...??

PETER. I went to join up – but they...

JESSIE. *(Interrupting.)* Why did you have to go and do that?

PETER. Will you let me finish...

JESSIE. *(Interrupting.)* Well that takes the bloody biscuit! You've sent the kids away, and now you want to go off and leave me on me own!

>   (*Pause as* **JESSIE** *waits for an answer. No reply.*)

I'm not being left a widow like your mam was.

PETER. That's not going to happen.

JESSIE. Your father thought that too – him and all the other Liverpool pals!

>   (**PETER** *is stung by her remark.*)

PETER. They wouldn't have me.

JESSIE. They wouldn't...?? What do you mean they wouldn't have you?

PETER. Medical grounds.

JESSIE. Medical grounds?

PETER. The old ticker doesn't meet the required standards.

JESSIE. Peter!

PETER. Apparently, I'm good enough to work down the docks – good enough to be a carter. I'm just not good enough to serve me country.

> (**PETER** *stares out of the window.* **JESSIE** *watches on.*)

JESSIE. Don't you be doing anything daft – do you hear me Peter?

> *(No reply.)*

(Louder.) Did you hear me Peter? I've got enough to worry about with the kids being so far away. I miss them and...

PETER. *(Interrupting.)* Do you think I don't miss them?

JESSIE. I didn't say that.

PETER. Do you think I wanted to send them away? Do you?

JESSIE. I just don't think that they're any safer in Wales and...

> *(He grabs his jacket and cap.)*

Where do you think you're going?

PETER. To the ale house – for a bit of bloody peace!

> *(He storms out.* **JESSIE** *calms herself. She looks at a family picture on the sideboard. The sight of her children in the picture*

prompts her to find a writing pad and a pencil. She sits to write to her children. She speaks as she writes. Another spotlight fades up on **JEAN**, **TOMMY** *and* **SHIRLEY** *grouped around the letter in Wales.* **JEAN** *and her mum* **JESSIE** *share the 'reading' as follows:)*

JESSIE. Dear Tommy, Shirley and Jean,

I was so pleased to get your letters last week. I'm sorry that I haven't replied sooner, but I wanted to put in some money for you to pass on to Mrs Griffiths in case she needs to buy you anything extra. Remember to give the money to her as soon as you get this letter. I hope that you are all still being good children for her and Mr Griffiths.

JEAN. It was lovely to hear how much you're enjoying Sunday school girls, and that Tommy has been picked for the school rugby team. We'll be cheering you on in Bootle Tommy. So let me know how you get on in your next letter home.

JESSIE. I've been busy knitting you all new jumpers, and some socks too. I'll send them on in a parcel next week. I just hope that you've all not grown too much and everything fits you properly.

JEAN. Uncle David is getting married soon. I'll send you a photograph of him and Teresa when I can. I'm sure David will look very handsome in his navy uniform, and Teresa will be a beautiful bride. It's a shame you girls won't be here to be bridesmaids but we'll all be thinking of you on the day.

JESSIE. Your dad and your nan send their best love and lots of hugs and kisses, and Prince sends a big cuddle too. He is still pulling the cart and keeping supplies going up and down the city. He's a good old lad and works really hard for us all.

JEAN. Always remember that we all love the three of you very very much, and really miss your hugs and kisses. So please give each other a big hug and pretend that it is Mum and Dad hugging you close. Will you do that for me? I can't wait for the day when we can all be together again.

JESSIE. Stay safe my little loves, and God Bless you all.

Your loving Mum.

> (*As* **JEAN**, **SHIRLEY** *and* **TOMMY** *obey their mum's wishes and hug each other in one huge loving hug,* **JESSIE** *folds the letter and places it in an envelope.*)

> (*Blackout.*)

Scene Nine – May 1940

(Sudden peal of church wedding bells. The wedding march plays as we see **DAVID** *in his navy uniform,* **TERESA** *dressed for her wedding day,* **PETER, JESSIE,** *Teresa's* **UNCLE EDDIE** *and* **AUNTY EILEEN,** *the Catholic priest and* **MAM.***)*

(A montage of wedding day poses.)

*(***MAM** *is stony-faced throughout.)*

(The focus shifts to the Liverpool Waterfront.)

(We hear a song in the style of Vera Lynn's "We'll Meet Again".*)

*(***TERESA** *stands tearfully waving* **DAVID** *off to sea.)*

(Lights fade on the scene.)

(Blackout.)

---

* A licence to produce *Waiting* does not include a performance licence for "We'll Meet Again". The publisher and author suggest that the licensee contact PRS to ascertain the music publisher and contact such music publisher to license or acquire permission for performance of the song. If a licence or permission is unattainable for "We'll Meet Again", the licensee may not use the song in *Waiting* but should create an original composition in a similar style or use a similar song in the public domain. For further information, please see the Music and Third-Party Materials Use Note on page iii.

Scene Ten – Summer 1940

(Bombing in Liverpool has been sporadic and the Christmas Blitz of 1940 has yet to hit the city.)

(A raucous local pub. **TERESA** *and* **EILEEN** *are sat with a drink listening to* **EDDIE** *who is entertaining the pub by crooning a popular love song of the time.***)*

*(***PETER** *and* **JESSIE** *enter with a full drink in their hand as* **EDDIE***'s song finishes.* **JESSIE***'s hair is up in a turban, and she wears overalls and boots underneath her coat.* **EILEEN** *notices* **JESSIE** *and waves her over.* **JESSIE** *joins her while* **PETER** *makes conversation with* **EDDIE** *and some other pub regulars.* **JESSIE** *quietly compares her own appearance with the more feminine attire of* **TERESA***.)*

EILEEN. Jessie! Over here love – come and join us.

*(***EILEEN** *pulls out a chair for* **JESSIE***.)*

JESSIE. Thanks Eileen.

EILEEN. That's it. Sit yourself down. You don't wanna be listening to that lot over there – it's all politics and football, football, football with them.

JESSIE. *(To* **TERESA***.)* Hello stranger. Long time no see.

TERESA. Hello.

JESSIE. Not seen you in here before.

---

* A licence to produce *Waiting* does not include a performance license for any third-party or copyrighted music. Licensees should create an original composition or use music in the public domain. For further information, please see the Music and Third-Party Materials Use Note on page iii.

TERESA. Eddie and Aunty Eileen asked me to come. I think they're feeling a bit sorry for me – you know – the poor war bride who's all on her ownsome.

EILEEN. You need a bit of fun Teresa. We all do. Isn't that right Jessie?

> (**JESSIE** *nods in agreement as the focus of the scene shifts to* **EDDIE** *and* **PETER** *who are deep in conversation about football.*)

EDDIE. Everton won't see his like again.

PETER. You're right there.

EDDIE. Dixie Dean. The man's a legend. A goal machine. I still can't believe that he's gone you know. That he's not at Everton anymore...

PETER. Get a grip will you. He hasn't died Eddie!

EDDIE. It just feels like it.

PETER. Mind you, Liverpool could do with a number nine like him.

EDDIE. True.

PETER. Half the team's joined up now, so it's bloody well decimated. And the strikers we've got left...Christ! They couldn't kick a ball down Brownlow Hill never mind hit the back of a net.

EDDIE. Hey – the last game I was at – a terrible missed penalty! It must have landed in Stanley Park. Liddle would have put it away no bother, or Tommy Lawton. That kid's a star alright. Only nineteen and he scored thirty-five goals in that last season before the war... thirty-five!

PETER. *(Interrupting.)* The glory days are over Eddie. We're all struggling now. All of us...

EDDIE. You're right lad. There's no getting away from the fact that most of the games now are an absolute bag of shite...

> *(As* **EDDIE** *utters this last line he is joined by* **EILEEN** *loudly finishing a sentence and the focus shifts back to the women.)*

EILEEN. ...bag of sugar! Couldn't believe my luck! You can't get it for love nor money at the moment. I've got a sweet tooth and this rationing's killing me!

JESSIE. I might pop round to yours and grab a cup for meself.

EILEEN. Do that. But don't spread the word. They'll all be wanting some.

JESSIE. *(Turns to* **TERESA.***)* You're quiet tonight girl. Have you heard from David lately?

TERESA. Not for a while.

JESSIE. When's he due home on leave?

TERESA. Soon I hope. It feels like he's been gone forever.

JESSIE. Like my babies...

EILEEN. How are the children Jessie?

JESSIE. Oh...alright. They write home...lovely little letters... But I still...you know... I miss them... *(She shrugs off her sadness.)* Anyhow – I've come out for a drink or two – you've gorra grab a little happiness while you can nowadays haven't you?

> *(The scene focus shifts back to* **PETER** *and* **EDDIE** *again.)*

EDDIE. I thought we'd have been hit more than we have by now.

PETER. Just be thankful Eddie.

EDDIE. Hey, I'm not complaining. Just saying...

PETER. It's mad down at the docks, non stop. The number of ships coming and going...just crazy. I've never grafted so hard in all me life. Nor has Jessie... She's bloody knackered but she's a trooper you know. I'm proud of her... I am...

(The scene focus shifts back to the women.)

TERESA. Have you come straight from work tonight?

(**JESSIE** *indicates her overalls.*)

JESSIE. How did you guess?

EILEEN. Where are you working now Jessie?

JESSIE. I'm doing shifts at the munitions factory, putting TNT into landmines.

TERESA. Jessie! That sounds dangerous.

EILEEN. They had women working in the munitions factories in the last war too.

JESSIE. Did you work there?

EILEEN. No. I managed to wangle a job with the Post Office while the lads were away in the last war. I've always been good at Maths and English, so passed the test. It was a big step up for me after coming across from Cork to Liverpool.

JESSIE. When did you leave Cork?

EILEEN. 1912. I was only eighteen you know. There was no work at home so all of us young uns were travelling – looking for a future. I started off as a domestic here, in one of those big Georgian Houses. Beautiful it was. Not that I saw much of it stuck in the kitchen all day! Two years peeling spuds and setting the fires every morning for the gentry was enough for me girls – so once the war started I was off! And the Post Office paid a lot better too...

JESSIE. You're right about the wages Eileen. My pay is a lot better now.

EILEEN. Men's jobs girls. Men's pay. And we do a better job than some men. Mind you – they're not all idle. I met Eddie there you know, when he came back from the war.

> (**EILEEN** *looks fondly across the room at* **EDDIE** *who is laughing at a joke someone has just told him.*)

TERESA. Anyway Jessie – I just hope that they're looking after you girls in munitions. It's a tough job you're doing.

> (**JESSIE** *takes a big gulp of her drink and sighs. She's knackered.*)

EILEEN. Rough day today?

> (**JESSIE** *nods.*)

JESSIE. Yeah. One of the girls – Avril – slipped on the floor with a can – ended up covered in red hot TNT. So they heaved her onto a trolley and got her down to the medical room straightaway.

TERESA. Is she alright?

JESSIE. She'll survive, but it was scary. She had to wait an hour for it to set before they could peel it off her.

TERESA. Oh my God!

JESSIE. Once they'd sorted her out she got straight back on the factory floor. That's Avril for you – as rough as hell but as hard as nails – hard as nails... She was raw – red raw. But do you know what she did when she got back on the line? She stood on a chair and shouted

"These are my Battle Scars!" ...That girl was my hero today... my hero... she deserves a bloody medal...

> (**JESSIE** *downs the rest of her drink as* **EDDIE** *shouts over to* **EILEEN** *to come and join him in a song. She feigns modesty, but* **TERESA**, **PETER** *and* **JESSIE** *encourage her to take the floor.* **PETER** *sits with* **JESSIE** *and* **TERESA** *as* **EDDIE** *and* **EILEEN** *sing a wartime favourite in the style of Billie Holliday.* * *They lead the pub in a full rendition of the song. It's tough for* **TERESA** *[missing David] and* **PETER** *and* **JESSIE** *[missing their children] to bear, but they join in regardless. The song ends to thunderous applause.)*

> (**JESSIE** *wipes away a tear.)*

That bloody song...it gets me every time...

> (*The last orders bell suddenly rings out.* **EDDIE** *shouts across to the table.)*

EDDIE. It's last orders! Any more for any more?

> (*They all raise their empty glasses.* **PETER** *shouts back.)*

PETER. Get 'em in Eddie lad. Get 'em in.

> (*Lights fade on the scene.)*

---

* A licence to produce *Waiting* does not include a performance licence for any third-party or copyrighted music. Licensees should create an original composition or use music in the public domain. For further information, please see the Music and Third-Party Materials Use Note on page iii.

Scene Eleven – November 1940

(In the darkness the sound of school children in the playground – a mix of Welsh and English voices.* Lights up on **JEAN** *playing hopscotch with* **SHIRLEY**. **JEAN** *finishes her turn.)*

JEAN. Your turn.

SHIRLEY. But I don't want to play hopscotch again.

JEAN. I thought you liked it.

SHIRLEY. Look – they're playing that new skipping game.

(She points to a group of girls in the distance.)

JEAN. Who is?

SHIRLEY. Siân and that lot over there.

*(***JEAN*** decides against it.)*

JEAN. Go and play with them if you want.

SHIRLEY. Aaaah come on Jean. Come with me.

*(***JEAN*** shakes her head.)*

*(***SHIRLEY*** hesitates.)*

JEAN. You go. I'll be alright.

*(***SHIRLEY*** exits. **JEAN** carries on with her lone game of hopscotch.)*

*(A rugby ball rolls into view. ***TOMMY*** runs onstage to retrieve it. He shouts offstage to* **OWEN**.)*

---

* The author encourages actors to use the Welsh dialogue in this scene, but an optional English translation is provided.

TOMMY. Na'i nol o Owen. [Nye knol o Owen.] / I'll get it Owen.

OWEN. *(Shouts offstage.)* Tafliad ni ydio cofia. [Tavliad knee udio covi.] / It's our throw in remember.

(**TOMMY** *throws the rugby ball offstage to* **OWEN.**)

TOMMY. *(Shouting.)* I! Ti Owen. [Ee! Tee Owen.] / Here! To you Owen.

OWEN. Dioch Tommy. Dewch hogia! [Deeolch Tommy. Dewch hoggia!] / Thanks Tommy. Come on lads!

(**TOMMY** *notices* **JEAN** *is on her own.*)

TOMMY. Alright our Jean?

JEAN. Yeah.

TOMMY. Where's Shirley?

JEAN. Over there – skipping with that lot over there.

TOMMY. Why aren't you playing with them?

(*No reply.*)

That Siân hasn't been bullying you again has she? Coz if she has I'll...

JEAN. *(Interrupting.)* She hasn't. Not since you told her.

TOMMY. Just belt her one if she starts. You've gorra stick up for yourself.

JEAN. I'm alright.

(**OWEN** *shouts from offstage.*)

OWEN. Dewch Tommy. [Dewch Tommy.] / Come on Tommy.

TOMMY. I'm coming! *(Repeats in Welsh.)* Dwi n dod. [Doeen dod.]

(He is stopped in his tracks by **JEAN**.*)*

JEAN. When will we go home Tommy?

*(***JEAN*** holds* **TOMMY**'*s gaze.)*

I miss Mam and Dad...

TOMMY. I know.

JEAN. How long will we have to wait to see them again?

(Pause.)

Do you think we'll see them this Christmas time Tommy? Do yer?

(Pause.)

TOMMY. I don't know Jean... I don't know...

*(***TOMMY*** picks up* **JEAN**'*s hopscotch stone for her, and hands it to her, holding her hand to comfort her as he does so.)*

Maybe we won't have to wait much longer and...

OWEN. Syma nei di Tommy! [Summa neigh dee Tommy!] / Get a move on will you Tommy!

*(***TOMMY*** gently pulls away, shouting to* **OWEN** *as he goes.)*

TOMMY. Dwi n dod Owen. [Doeen dod Owen.] / I'm coming Owen.

*(***JEAN*** resumes her solitary game of hopscotch, singing to herself.)*

JEAN.
THE BIG SHIP SAILS ON THE ALLY ALLY OH
THE ALLY ALLY OH, THE ALLY ALLY OH
THE BIG SHIP SAILS ON THE ALLY ALLY OH
ON THE LAST DAY OF SEPTEMBER

JEAN.

> THE CAPTAIN SAID IT WILL NEVER NEVER DO
> NEVER NEVER DO, NEVER NEVER DO
> THE CAPTAIN SAID IT WILL NEVER NEVER DO
> ON THE LAST DAY OF SEPTEMBER...

> *(Lights fade on the scene.)*

> *(Blackout.)*

Scene Twelve – Early December 1940

(Night. A battleship deck. Mid Atlantic. The sound of ocean waves hitting the ship.)

*(**DAVID** is having a smoke. He takes a picture of Teresa out of his breast pocket and gazes at it before reading her accompanying letter. We see an image of **TERESA** as we hear her speaking the words.)*

TERESA. My dear David,

I miss you so much, and Christmas is going to be hard without you – wherever you are.

It's scary, not knowing where you are. If I could at least put a finger on a map and say "There. There. THAT'S where he is tonight," I'd track it every night, and put little pins in the map, watching them getting nearer and nearer to Liverpool. And when that pin hits Liverpool I'll be down on that quay waiting for you to jump ship straight into my arms. But that's all a dream for now.

It's grim here at the moment, and there's no denying it. All the shops have got black paper on their windows, and when that horrible siren goes all the lights go out. Durning Road shelter got hit a while back. So many people dead, so suddenly. Thankfully it's all been quiet since then.

I bumped into Jessie last week. The kids are still fine in Wales. But I've not seen your mam. She's just too scary for me on my own. We'll have to visit her together next time you're home.

Come home soon David. If I'd realised how long I'd have to wait to see you again, I'd have held on to you as hard as I could and never let you go.

Stay safe sweetheart.

TERESA. All my love and kisses,

Teresa

> (**DAVID** *places the letter safely back in his pocket. He has a final drag on his cigarette.*)
>
> (*He visibly winces as the distant sound of enemy fire suddenly grows louder and more menacing. Light snaps off* **DAVID**.)
>
> (*Blackout.*)

Scene Thirteen – December 1940
Christmas time

(A stained glass window lights up the stage. **TOMMY**, **JEAN** *and* **SHIRLEY** *stand with the chapel congregation singing "Silent Night" in Welsh.* *They are oblivious to the sound of bombers overhead slowly increasing in volume as the carol is sung.)*

TOMMY, JEAN & SHIRLEY.
DAWEL NÔS, SANCTAIDD YW'R NÔS
CWSG A GERDD, WAUN A RHÔS,
ETO'N EFFRO MAE JOSEFF A MAIR;
FABAN ANNWYL YNGHWSG YN Y GWAIR,
CWSG MEWN GWYNFYD A HEDD
CWSG MEWN GWYNFYD A HEDD

DAWEL NÔS, SANCTAIDD YW'R NÔS
WELE FRY SEREN DLOS;
DAW'S BUGEILIOG A'R DOETHION I'R DRWS;
FABAN ANNWYL,YR WYT TI MOR DLWS,
CWSG MEWN GWYNFYD A HEDD,
CWSG MEWN GWYNFYD A HEDD.

(A huge explosion suddenly shatters a stained glass window in Liverpool.)

(The Liverpool Christmas Blitz has started.)

*(***MAM** *hammers on the front door of Peter and Jessie's home.)*

MAM. Jessie! Are you in there? Open the door. Open the door!

---

* In the original production "Silent Night" was sung in Welsh. This can also be sung in English.

(Inside the house **JESSIE** *is cowering under the table, her hands over her ears. The screech of a descending bomb.)*

*(***MAM*** *peers in through the window.)*

MAM. Jessie. JESSIE!

(No response.)

The back door – the back door...

(She rushes off to try and access the house via the back alley.)

(Bombs continue to rain down.)

*(***MAM*** *charges into the darkened room, looking around her.)*

(There is a momentary lull in the bombing.)

JESSIE. *(Eyes tight shut, babbling a prayer to herself.)* Our father who art in heaven, hallowed be thy name...

*(***MAM*** *realises the sound is coming from under the table. She kneels and crawls to* **JESSIE**, *slowly prising* **JESSIE**'s *hands away from her ears.)*

MAM. Jessie... Jessie love...it's me...

*(***JESSIE*** *finally opens her eyes.)*

(They cling to each other as the air raid rages on.)

(Light fades on the kitchen scene.)

(Lights up on the stable yard which is ablaze.)

(Pandemonium. Horses in distress.)

(**PETER** *runs in and grabs the reins/bridle for his horse.*)

(*The bombing is reaching a climax.*)

PETER. (*Shouts.*) PRINCE!

(*Lights fade on Liverpool scenes and focus again on the Welsh chapel.*)

(*The volume of the carol increases as the sound of the bombing fades out.* **TOMMY**, **JEAN** *and* **SHIRLEY** *finish singing the last verse of* "*Silent Night*".)

(*Momentary silence.*)

(*Blackout.*)

End of Act One

Interval

ACT TWO

Scene One – December 1940
The Christmas Blitz continues

(A light-and-soundscape of the Blitz – an assault on the senses.)

(Air raid sirens blare out.)

(A red glow fills the stage as the soundscape unfolds.)

(The sound of bombers overhead.)

(Bombs rain down.)

(Buildings crumble.)

(People shouting and running for shelter.)

(Firehoses raining water down onto the buildings.)

(Rescuers excavating the rubble for survivors.)

(The sound of the bombers recedes into the night.)

(The fires fade.)

(The all clear siren sounds.)

Scene Two – 23rd December 1940
End of the Christmas Blitz

*(Early dawn. Lights up on **PETER** on bombed out streets in Liverpool. He is filthy. Exhausted, he sits to have a quiet fag.)*

*(Teresa's **UNCLE EDDIE**, equally dishevelled and a fellow rescuer, enters.)*

*(**PETER** silently offers him a fag. They sit and smoke, a brief respite from the horrors of the night before.)*

*(**EDDIE** finally breaks the silence.)*

EDDIE. Frigging Nazi bastards.

PETER. You're right there.

EDDIE. Do you think Hitler's got a personal grudge against scousers?

PETER. He doesn't like us that's for sure.

(Pause.)

EDDIE. I'm knackered.

PETER. And me.

EDDIE. Do you realise that we've hardly been home for three days?

PETER. Mmmm.

*(**PETER** goes to light another fag and can't because his hand is shaking. **EDDIE** lights the fag for him.)*

Dunno what's the matter with me...

EDDIE. It'll pass. I'm the same lad... And hey – forget the fucking Luftwaffe – those bloody rats frightened me to death last night!

(**PETER** *laughs.*)

PETER. I saw you jump a mile.

EDDIE. Christ Almighty! Size of cats – and tails as long as washing lines.

(*Pause as they survey the scene.*)

The state of it all. You wouldn't know where one street ends and another begins.

(**PETER** *nods as they have a few more puffs on their fags.*)

They won't be reporting all this in the newspapers or the radio though will they? They never do. London'll get all the glory.

PETER. S'pose they've got to keep it quiet – you know – not let the Germans know how much damage they're doing.

EDDIE. Do me a bloody favour lad. It won't be a secret in Nazi HQ. They've got a bird's eye view of what they're doing – we've been lit up like a frigging bonfire every night!

PETER. True.

(*Pause.*)

EDDIE. Fire... Now that's a terrible way to go...

PETER. I've seen enough of that to last a lifetime.

EDDIE. Those firemen...

PETER. Fearless.

EDDIE. Mind you, you did well digging down in that tunnel last night to rescue that lass.

PETER. I felt like I'd escaped from the grave by the time I got her back out again.

(Pause.)

EDDIE. Shame her fellah didn't make it.

PETER. It didn't seem right, leaving him there. He'll not get a proper burial.

EDDIE. We can't do it all lad. And the word is that the corpy are having problems burying the bodies anyway. No sooner do they get one hole dug and another funeral party turns up... Thank God the British are good at queueing!

(Another puff on their fags.)

That screaming noise the bombs make...

PETER. Makes my hair stand on end.

EDDIE. They say you never hear the one that's got your name on it. It just lands on top of you and 'puff' – you go up in smoke... Talking of smokes – can I cadge another fag?

*(**PETER** hands **EDDIE** another fag.)*

The ladies'll be handing out the tea and sandwiches soon.

PETER. Oh aye.

EDDIE. Yeah... Have you seen that gal that wears the trousers! They definitely show off her best asset... Yep... I'm gonna hang around for that cuppa tea before I call it a night.

PETER. It's morning Eddie.

EDDIE. Is it? ...Oh aye... So it is... You walking home?

PETER. Yeah. Got to check on Prince first. We've moved the horses. Put up some temporary stables.

EDDIE. I could do with a horse meself. Went to ride the tram home the other day and there it was – flipped over on its side on the corner of Lime Street. Bloody broken glass everywhere.

(The all clear siren sounds again.)

PETER. That's the all clear. I'm off. Look after yourself.

EDDIE. You too. Hey – I'll ask that judy for a drop of whisky in me tea this morning instead of milk. That should raise a laugh! I think she fancies me you know – but don't tell Eileen!

*(**PETER** looks the bedraggled **EDDIE** up and down.)*

PETER. D'yer reckon?

EDDIE. She's got a lovely smile. And one of them posh voices. I like that. A posh tart. Right up my street.

*(**PETER** laughs.)*

PETER. She won't be able to resist you in that get up!

EDDIE. Look who's talking! You get yourself a bloody bath when you get home – you look like a frigging chimney sweep!

*(**PETER** points to himself and then at the equally filthy **EDDIE**.)*

PETER. Pot – kettle – kettle – black.

*(**PETER** laughs and exits. **EDDIE** hears the sound of rattling tea cups.)*

POSH WOMAN'S VOICE. *(Offstage.)* Tea's ready Boys! Come and get it!

(**EDDIE** *adjusts his grubby appearance.*)

EDDIE. Coming my love... Coming!

(**EDDIE** *sings his and Eileen's favourite love song to himself as he exits.**)

(*Blackout.*)

---

* A licence to produce *Waiting* does not include a performance licence for any third-party or copyrighted music. Licensees should create an original composition or use music in the public domain. For further information, please see the Music and Third-Party Materials Use Note on page iii.

Scene Three – December 1940
After the Christmas Blitz

(Lights up on Peter and Jessie's home. **MAM** *is sat clutching her broken teapot, and the framed picture of Jim which has miraculously survived the bombing of her home.)*

*(***JESSIE*** enters with a cup of tea for them both. The song fades out.)*

JESSIE. Not too much milk in your tea. Just how you like it.

(No reply.)

Amy?

*(***MAM*** sighs, and brandishes the offending teapot.)*

MAM. Me best china! Look at it! Everything's gone...or broken...all of it...except this... *(Holding up the picture of Jim.)* Jim...it's all I've got left of him...

(She hugs Jim's portrait tight.)

JESSIE. You'll carry Jim with you forever Amy – in your heart.

(No reply.)

Amy?

(Long pause.)

MAM. I HATE them bloody Germans!

JESSIE. *(Sadly.)* So do I.

MAM. I wish I was a man. I do. I'd shoot the flaming lot of them!

(They sip their tea.)

JESSIE. Are you going to be alright in that back bedroom? The bed's a bit small and...

MAM. *(Interrupting.)* I don't want to be any bother.

JESSIE. You're no bother.

MAM. I don't know how long I'll be here Jessie so...

JESSIE. *(Interrupting.)* Stop fretting will yer. You're with us now.

> (**MAM** *struggles with her feelings, refusing to let the tears flow.*)

MAM. Did you notice Jessie, when we went to my house today, well – what's left of it – did you notice that bowl of tinned peaches was still where I'd left it – on that ledge in the kitchen? Covered in broken glass it was – and all that soot from the fire – absolutely filthy.

JESSIE. Mmmmmm.

MAM. A tragedy. That's what it is. A tragedy! *(Pause.)* ...I doubt I'll be able to get any more peaches till after the war.

JESSIE. S'pose so.

> (**MAM** *pulls her ration book out of her pocket and brandishes it.*)

MAM. At least I've still got me ration book! At least that didn't get burnt too! Bloody rationing! I join any flaming queue I see now if I'm out and about. Just the other day there was a long queue outside Jeffries – all for a few onions – all for a couple of flaming onions! Mind you – I was glad of 'em.

JESSIE. More tea?

MAM. *(Still ranting on and not listening.)* And Ted Dooley's house. You know him...two doors down from mine. A bomb came straight through his roof and landed inside the piano. Didn't go off! Not a tickle on the ivories! Who'd have ever thought that could happen? The bomb squad defused it and took it away.

JESSIE. The bomb?

MAM. Mmmm...shame it wasn't the piano. He can't play for toffee.

> (**JESSIE** *stifles a laugh.*)

You know why pianos were invented don't you?

JESSIE. No.

MAM. So the player's got somewhere to put his pint glass. And that's Ted's problem. He only plays when he's been drinking – so he misses half the notes. Terrible!

> (*They both manage to giggle now.* **JESSIE** *gathers the tea cups.*)

JESSIE. Are you having another cuppa? I can top up the pot with some hot water that's left.

MAM. Oh go on then.

> (**JESSIE** *forages in her pocket for the latest letters from the children.*)

JESSIE. Here. I haven't had a chance to show you these letters yet. From the children. It's so lovely to hear from them.

> (**JESSIE** *exits with the teacups.* **MAM** *opens the letters. Lights fade to a spot on* **MAM** *in the Wright household as we see and hear* **JEAN**, **SHIRLEY** *and* **TOMMY** *in Wales writing their letters home. One child's letter merges into another's.*)

JEAN. Dear Mam and Dad. We have just got back from Chapel.

SHIRLEY. It's like Church in England, but we sing in Welsh...

TOMMY. Sometimes we go three times on Sundays – which is a bit boring.

SHIRLEY. Sundays are the best for dinners.

TOMMY. Mrs Griffiths is a good cook, but not as good as you are Mam.

JEAN. I gave that last pound you sent to her, and she said to say Thank You.

TOMMY. Do you know that I can speak Welsh really good now!

JEAN. I think our Tommy knows some Welsh swear words but I'm not sure.

SHIRLEY. We sometimes have lamb for dinner. Did you know that a lamb is a baby sheep?

TOMMY. On Sundays we have potatoes, carrots and peas, and gravy with our dinner.

SHIRLEY. Sunday dinner is really yummy.

JEAN. I was a bit scared when we first came here because I couldn't understand everyone. But I'm happier now Mam, and I have made some new friends. So please don't worry about me too much.

TOMMY. I'm learning the names of all the birds. Owen said that we'll see kingfishers on the river when it's warmer in the spring.

SHIRLEY. I am still taking good care of Victoria. I hug her every night in bed and pretend it's you Mam.

TOMMY. Some of the horses up at the farm are as big as Prince, but not as handsome. I still want to work with Dad at the stables when I come back home.

JEAN. I'm helping Tommy and Shirley as much as I can with their schoolwork.

TOMMY & SHIRLEY. Our Jean has helped me write this because her spelling is better than mine.

TOMMY. I can't wait to show Dad how good I am now at playing rugby.

JEAN. I really missed having a slice of Nan's Christmas cake.

TOMMY. I hope she's saved us some.

ALL. I can't wait to see you all again. Lots of love from…

TOMMY. Tommy.

JEAN. Jean.

SHIRLEY. Victoria and Shirley.

> (*Spot fades on* **JEAN**, **SHIRLEY** *and* **TOMMY**.)

> (**MAM** *hugs the letters close.*)

MAM. Keep them safe and well God. Keep them safe and well…

> (*For the first time since her house was bombed, she cries.*)

> (*Lights fade on the scene.*)

> (*Blackout.*)

Scene Four – February 1941

(Wales. A cold winter's day.)

(The sound of children playing on their way home from school.)

*(**JEAN**, **SHIRLEY** and **TOMMY** are near the river which is frozen over.)*

*(**TOMMY** bends down to touch the ice.)*

TOMMY. Bet I could slide right across the river today.

SHIRLEY. Could yer?

TOMMY. Yeah. Right to the other side.

JEAN. You can't swim.

TOMMY. Neither can you!

JEAN. None of us can!

TOMMY. You don't need to swim anyway.

> *(He takes a step out and stamps his foot hard a couple of times.)*

Look! It's iced over. It's solid.

> *(**JEAN** grabs **SHIRLEY**'s hand.)*

JEAN. You're being stupid Tommy. Come on Shirley. We'll be late home for our tea.

> *(**SHIRLEY** pulls away from her.)*

SHIRLEY. But I want to slide across too.

JEAN. No you don't. There's the bridge over there. Let's just use that like we normally do.

(**TOMMY** *takes another step to test the ice and then jumps up and down.*)

Don't Tommy!

TOMMY. (*Laughing.*) It's alright. I saw Owen and Morgan slide right across it last night on the way home from school.

SHIRLEY. Shall we do it Jean? Shall we?

(**JEAN** *grabs* **SHIRLEY**'*s hand again.*)

JEAN. No!

(**TOMMY** *takes off – gaining speed and hollering with joy as he slides on the ice. He shouts from the other side of the river.*)

TOMMY. It's easy Jean. Come on! Come on Shirley.

(**JEAN** *is not convinced.* **SHIRLEY** *escapes her grasp.*)

JEAN. No Shirley. NO!

(*Too late.* **SHIRLEY** *is already on the ice, giggling as she slides along.*)

SHIRLEY. It's easy Jean.

TOMMY. (*Offstage.*) Come on Shirley. You can do it!

SHIRLEY. I'm coming. I'm coming.

(*As* **SHIRLEY** *reaches the middle of the river there is an ominous cracking sound. She stops. Silence. Then another ominous crack in the ice.*)

JEAN. Stay there. Don't move. STAY THERE!

(**JEAN** *sinks on her knees to scramble to* **SHIRLEY**. *She moves her little sister back*

in the direction from which she has come.
SHIRLEY *gingerly walks back.)*

JEAN. That's it Shirley. Just slowly...slowly...slowly. You'll
be alright. Don't run – that's it.

(**JEAN** *watches on.* **SHIRLEY** *reaches solid
ground and turns to* **JEAN**.)

SHIRLEY. *(Softly crying.)* Come on our Jean. Come on...

*(We hear another huge crack in the ice.
Blackout.)*

*(In the blackout we hear an echoing shout
from* **TOMMY**.)*

TOMMY. JEAN!

Scene Five – February 1941

(In the blackout a funeral bell tolls, and continues to do so throughout this sequence.)

(We see **JESSIE**, **PETER**, **TOMMY**, **SHIRLEY** *and* **MAM** *wearing funereal black as though in an old black and white photograph.)*

(Stillness.)

*(***PETER*** *has his arm around* **TOMMY** *to comfort him.)*

*(***MAM*** *holds* **SHIRLEY***'s hand.)*

*(***JESSIE*** *stands alone in her grief.)*

(She takes a step forward, a handful of earth in her hand.)

(She stares into the abyss of Jean's grave, and slowly lets the soil run through her hands. She remains rooted to the spot.)

(The bell still tolls.)

(Blackout.)

Scene Six – February 1941

> *(Lights up on the Wright family home.*
> **PETER**, **JESSIE** *and* **MAM** *enter still in funeral
> dress. They have just travelled back from
> Wales. The children are not with them.* **PETER**
> *breaks the silence.)*

PETER. I'll take this upstairs then.

> *(**PETER** exits with the suitcase.)*

MAM. That was kind of Mrs Griffiths' family to put us up
for the night wasn't it?

> *(No reply.)*

She seems a lovely woman. Very hospitable.

> *(Still no reply.)*

> *(**PETER** enters.)*

PETER. Jessie love, I…

> *(**JESSIE** ignores him and sweeps out of
> the room.)*

MAM. Give her a bit of time eh love?

PETER. Yeah…

> *(Pause.)*

I didn't want to leave them there Mam.

MAM. I know.

PETER. But how can I bring them back?

MAM. I know son.

PETER. Our Tommy…he thinks it was all his fault.

MAM. Poor lad.

PETER. As soon as the bombing stops I'm bringing them home. I am... I've just gorra wait until...

> *(He is interrupted by* **JESSIE** *entering the room.* **MAM** *rises.)*

MAM. Well – I'm off to bed. That train journey seemed to go on forever didn't it?

> *(***MAM** *kisses* **PETER** *on the cheek.)*

(To **PETER.***)* Goodnight love. *(To* **JESSIE.***)* Try and get some rest eh?

> *(She squeezes* **JESSIE**'s *hand and exits.)*

> *(A long silence.)*

JESSIE. You had to have your own way again didn't you?

PETER. Jessie, I...

JESSIE. *(Interrupting.)* You had to leave them there didn't you?

PETER. I didn't want to...

JESSIE. *(Interrupting.)* They'll be safer there than here you said.

PETER. Look love, all I can say is...

JESSIE. *(Interrupting.)* You've had your say Peter! When you shipped them all off to Wales with those gas masks round their necks. You...you and the flaming government...you all had your say then. Well I'm having mine now. Do you hear me? I'm having my bloody say right now – because it wasn't safe was it Peter? Not like you said it would be... I know Mrs Griffiths is a lovely woman...and I know that the bombs aren't falling on them out there. But no-one will ever look after our kids like we can. Not like us...not like me. I'm her mum. And I wasn't there. I wasn't there!

PETER. Jessie, it was an accident.

(She turns on him with a vengeance.)

JESSIE. I said to you that if anything happened to our kids, to MY kids.

*(**JESSIE** breaks down. He goes to comfort her.)*

PETER. Jessie love, come here will yer.

JESSIE. Don't touch me...don't...

(She pushes him away and rushes from the room.)

*(**PETER** stands alone.)*

(Blackout.)

Scene Seven – March 1941

(The Stables. The sound of Prince and other horses settling down for the night. His work and his horse are **PETER**'s *solace now. He is cleaning the horse tack – a nightly ritual.* **TERESA** *enters.)*

TERESA. Peter?

PETER. Teresa? What brings you here?

TERESA. This.

(She hands him a letter.)

It's from David. He sent it to my address by mistake.

PETER. Thanks.

TERESA. I haven't got the courage to pop round to your house with your mam there. I know she's living with you and Jessie now, so I just thought I'd... I just wanted you to have it.

PETER. Her bark's worse than her bite you know.

TERESA. Is that a fact.

PETER. She'd be pleased to see you.

TERESA. Hmmm...

PETER. You probably hear from our David a damn sight more than she does at the moment. She'd be glad to hear the news – any news – about him.

*(***TERESA** *nods.)*

TERESA. Anyway... I'd best be off.

(She turns to go.)

PETER. Don't...don't go... stay... talk for a while...if you want to.

(She sits and watches him work. Eventually...)

TERESA. I'm so sorry about what happened to Jean.

*(**PETER** carries on cleaning the tack.)*

PETER. She's a...she was...a good girl...

(He works as he talks.)

Best reader in the school you know.

(Pause.)

I miss that... her reading to me... she loved doing that... showing off the long words she'd learned in school that day.

TERESA. She was a lovely girl Peter.

(Pause.)

PETER. I thought I was protecting her.

TERESA. I know.

PETER. But I wasn't was I?

TERESA. You mustn't blame yourself.

PETER. When she was in real danger...I wasn't there...

*(Long pause as **PETER** carries on working. **TERESA** breaks the silence.)*

TERESA. I know that you've been out firefighting a lot with my Uncle Eddie. You're all so brave...you must be shattered and...

PETER. *(Interrupting.)* I AM <u>NOT</u> BRAVE!... I'm just getting on with it...just getting on with it like everyone else... And waiting – God only knows how sick to my stomach I am of waiting – waiting for those bombs to fall...shaking in me boots knowing that this night might be the last... I am so bloody sick of waiting for an end to it all... But what else can I do eh? What else can we all do?...I'm not brave Teresa – I'm just hanging on for dear life, just like we all are...

(*Pause.*)

I'm sorry... I shouldn't have... sorry...

(*Silence as* **PETER** *tidies away his work tools.*)

TERESA. You're a good man Peter. You and David. You're both good men.

(*Pause.*)

PETER. How is he?

TERESA. Desperate to get home again. I can't believe I haven't seen him since late September.

PETER. It's a shame he couldn't get to see everyone.

TERESA. It was all so last minute. A flying visit. I was dead chuffed to see him, but...waving goodbye to him at the docks... Sometimes it feels like everyone's leaving Liverpool behind.

(*Pause.*)

Eddie and Eileen are very kind but... I miss him, even more now that I know that I'm... (*She stops herself from finishing the sentence.*) Listen to me rabbitting away... you don't wanna be listening to me going on and on...

PETER. Hey – I'd happily listen to you all night so don't you be worrying about that.

(*He resumes working.*)

TERESA. How's Jessie?

(**PETER** *chooses not to answer.*)

TERESA. And Tommy and Shirley – they're staying in
Wales then?

PETER. *(He nods.)* They are. I know it's a bit quieter now,
but you've only got to look across the Mersey to see
Birkenhead and Wallasey getting hammered. I see
those flares going up and that blood red sky... it'll be
our turn again soon.

>   *(***TERESA*** *nods in agreement. Then she checks*
>   *her watch and sighs.)*

TERESA. Oh no. Look at the time. I'll have to go. I've got to
catch the tram. And I hate being on them late at night
now. No lights on. It's just like riding a ghost train...
Oh! I'm sorry... I didn't think... what a stupid thing to
say... I didn't mean... anyway... look after yourself.

>   *(She tentatively touches his shoulder. They*
>   *end up in a mutual long and tender farewell*
>   *hug – both missing their partners and taking*
>   *physical comfort in each other.)*

PETER. Stay safe Teresa.

TERESA. And you Peter. And you...

>   *(She exits.* ***PETER*** *opens David's letter.)*

>   *(A spot comes up on* ***DAVID*** *speaking the*
>   *words.)*

DAVID. Dear Peter,

I'm sorry I've taken so long to write to you these last
few months. We've had a lot of work to get through,
and I'm not allowed to tell you exactly where we are,
but at least the snow is starting to disappear and I'm
not freezing in my bunk any more. Sometimes it feels
like all we're doing is hanging around waiting for
something to kick off, but it's all starting to look a bit

lively now and I think we might see some real action again soon.

(Pause...)

I find it hard to write letters home at the best of times. And this is not the best of times. It's the worst. What can I say to you about our Jean except I haven't stopped thinking about her since I got the news. You know I'm not religious, but I hope there's a special place for her in heaven, and that she's sat up there on a cloud with our dad, looking down and wanting to protect us all. I'll always remember her as a sweet and kind girl, and a really bright spark. It's hard to believe that she's really gone. God only knows how many tears you've shed. I know I cried buckets when I got the news.

I don't suppose that Teresa has told you that she's expecting. The baby's due in May, and we'd like to name the little one after Jean – if we have a girl that is. I know it's a lot to ask so have a think about it, and hopefully we can raise a glass to our Jean's memory next time I'm home.

It's been too long since my feet stood on solid ground.

Until we meet again.

Your brother,

David

> *(The sound of distant enemy fire grows louder.)*

> *(Blackout.)*

Scene Eight–April 1941

> (*Lights fade up on the Wright home.* **MAM**
> *is ready for bed in her nightdress and is*
> *adjusting her hair net.* **JESSIE** *enters.*)

MAM. I'm off to bed in a minute love. Just warming this
brick in the fire. Nice and toasty for me feet.

JESSIE. Good idea.

MAM. You'd think things would be a bit warmer by now
– but spring nights! Brrrr. They can still be a bit chilly
can't they?

> (**JESSIE** *picks up her knitting.*)

I've always suffered with cold feet. Used to warm them
on my Jim in bed. He had lovely warm legs. (*She smiles
to herself.*) He used to say that I was like a vampire
sucking the warmth out of them every night... I still
miss the silly old fool...and his legs.

> (*No reply from* **JESSIE** *who busies herself with*
> *her knitting.*)

Is our Peter out fire watching again tonight?

JESSIE. Yes.

> (**MAM** *folds the brick in an old towel.*)

MAM. Well – things have been a bit quieter these last few
weeks – so let's hope he's not out too late eh?

JESSIE. Mmmm.

> (*Pause.*)

MAM. Do you ever get cold feet in bed Jessie?

JESSIE. Pardon?

MAM. I said – do you get cold feet in bed?

JESSIE. Sometimes... yes... sometimes.

MAM. Mmmmm...so what do you do about it?

JESSIE. What do you mean?

MAM. What do you do about your cold feet?

JESSIE. I'm not sure what you...

MAM. Because you're not warming them on Peter's legs that's for sure.

JESSIE. Eh?

(**MAM** *stares her out.*)

MAM. Because if he's sleeping down here and *(She points to the ceiling.)* you're sleeping up there – your feet must be like blocks of ice by now. It's gone on for too long and...

JESSIE. *(Interrupting.)* Hold on a minute Amy! I don't think that it's any of your business...

MAM. *(Interrupting.)* Any of my business? Really?

JESSIE. You heard me.

MAM. My son's happiness isn't any of my business?

JESSIE. I don't have to listen to this...

(**JESSIE** *starts to storm out of the room.*)

MAM. If you want my advice Jessie...

JESSIE. *(Interrupting.)* If I want your advice Amy I'll bloody well ask for it!

MAM. When I ask if you want my advice it's just me being polite! It doesn't matter if you want it or not coz you're going to get it anyway. So sit down!

(**JESSIE** *reluctantly sits.*)

That's better.

(Pause. They both calm down.)

MAM. Look love, the fact of the matter is that you can't go on blaming Peter for what happened to Jean.

(No reply.)

Can't you see that Jessie? It's just not fair.

(Still no reply.)

I know what it's like to lose someone. I lost my Jim all those years ago, but that was different. He was a grown man and...it's just different. No-one ever thinks they're going to bury their own child, and I don't pretend to know how you must feel losing your Jean. I only know that she's in my thoughts every day, and that I pray for you. God only knows how much I've prayed for you to choose to be happy again one day...because you have to you know... you have to start allowing yourself some happiness Jessie. Because if you don't, then you've died too. And it won't be just Jean that you've lost, you'll lose Peter too, your family... you'll lose everything.

The most important thing you can do now for our Tommy and Shirley is to love their dad as much as you love them – believe me – it is. Let Peter back into your heart Jessie, for your sake – for all of you – for Tommy and Shirley... let Peter warm your feet up in bed again.

(Pause.)

Jessie?

*(**MAM** gathers up the brick in the towel.)*

Goodnight love.

*(**MAM** goes to leave, **JESSIE** finally speaks.)*

JESSIE. Amy...

MAM. Yes?

JESSIE. Nothing... nothing. Goodnight.

> (**MAM** *exits.* **JESSIE** *ponders on what* **MAM** *has said. She resumes her knitting. Time passes. We hear the ticking of the clock. She falls asleep in the chair.* **PETER** *enters the room. He gently wakes her.*)

PETER. Jessie... Jessie.

> (*She stirs.*)

It's late.

JESSIE. Busy night?

PETER. Not so bad – things were easing off so we've got off early.

JESSIE. You must be parched. I'll make you a cuppa.

PETER. No, no...you go on up. Get some sleep. I can look after meself down here.

> (*Pause.*)

JESSIE. I could bring it up to you...if you like...

PETER. Sorry?

JESSIE. Bring your cup of tea up to you...in bed...if you like.

PETER. Our bed?

JESSIE. Our bed – yes...

> (*Pause. They understand each other.*)

PETER. Yes...yeah... I'd like that Jessie...if you're sure.

JESSIE. I'm sure Peter.

> (*She gently eases off his jacket, and takes his cap off. She tenderly smooths his hair.*)

JESSIE. You go on up then love.

PETER. Right...

>   *(He pauses at the door. They exchange looks.)*

JESSIE. I won't be long.

>   (**PETER** *exits.* **JESSIE** *lovingly hugs his jacket and cap to her.)*

>   *(Blackout.)*

Scene Nine – May 1941

(**TERESA** *is in her nightie and dressing gown, and is sat in a darkened maternity wing of the Mill Road Infirmary in Liverpool. She holds her baby in her arms, and is trying to soothe her back to sleep. Her* **AUNTY EILEEN** *is with her.*)

MATRON'S VOICE. *(Offstage.)* Alright ladies. Visiting time's over so start saying your goodnights to your babies if you can. You all need a good night's sleep as much as they do don't forget...so I'll be back to check on you all in five minutes...

EILEEN. *(Coos over the baby...)* Sounds like I've got me marching orders from Matron! I'll be off then love, and I'll make sure that telegram gets sent off to David tomorrow.

TERESA. Thanks Aunty Eileen.

EILEEN. He'll be chuffed to bits to hear the news.

TERESA. He will!

EILEEN. Try and get a good night's sleep. I'll see you tomorrow.

(**EILEEN** *kisses* **TERESA** *goodbye and leaves.* **TERESA** *rocks the baby.*)

TERESA. Come on now Jean. That was the Matron speaking! Time to close those lovely blue eyes or the old dragon will be back nagging us again in a few minutes...

(The baby starts to settle a bit.)

That's better... you're such a good girl Jean. Such a good girl. Yes you are! And I can't wait for your daddy to meet you! Look, we've got a letter from him today...

(She holds up the letter to show baby Jean, and then tucks it into the baby's shawl for safekeeping.)

TERESA. He doesn't know that you've arrived yet, but he soon will. Your Great Aunt Eileen will be sending him a telegram tomorrow telling him all about you. I can't wait for him to sail back home again to meet you... I can't wait...

*(**TERESA** softly sings Jean to sleep with a lullaby.)*

MY BONNIE LIES OVER THE OCEAN
MY BONNIE LIES OVER THE SEA
MY BONNIE LIES OVER THE OCEAN
OH, BRING BACK MY BONNIE TO ME

BRING BACK, BRING BACK
OH, BRING BACK YOUR DADDY TO ME, TO ME
BRING BACK, BRING BACK
OH, BRING BACK YOUR DADDY TO ME

O BLOW YE WINDS OVER THE OCEAN
O BLOW YE WINDS OVER THE SEA
O BLOW YE WINDS OVER THE OCEAN
TO BRING BACK YOUR DADDY TO ME

BRING BACK, BRING BACK
OH, BRING BACK YOUR DADDY TO ME, TO ME
BRING BACK, BRING BACK
OH, BRING BACK YOUR DADDY TO ME

(A moment's contented silence and complete stillness. Then a sudden earth-shattering blast as a German bomb scores a direct hit on the maternity ward and Mill Road Hospital.)

(Blackout.)

(Air raid sirens blare out in the darkness and sounds of the city being attacked with full force from the air. The bombing continues...)

Scene Ten – May 1941

(Bombs are still raining down on the city.)

(Lights come up on **MAM** *and* **JESSIE** *in a dark air raid shelter. Both are dressed in night attire underneath their coats/scarves, and have their gas masks with them. As the sound of the Blitz still reverberates, they build a makeshift bed with the blankets and the pillows. They settle down for the night, huddling together for comfort and warmth. The sound of the Blitz fades a little.* **MAM** *surveys the scene.)*

MAM. We're like a load of bloody sardines in this bomb shelter.

JESSIE. Safer than in the house Mam.

MAM. I'd rather die in me own bed!

JESSIE. No you wouldn't.

MAM. I would! I'm sick of the bloody Luftwaffe dictating where I'm gonna sleep for the night.

(They huddle together for comfort as the bombing intensifies. **JESSIE** *quietly sobs and* **MAM** *hugs her close.)*

Hey, hey – come here Jessie. Come here. We'll be alright. We will.

JESSIE. It's Peter I'm scared for – he's still out there with Eddie and the others lads. I don't know where they get the strength from... I'm always scared he won't make it home after a night like this.

MAM. So am I love, but you'd be wrong to hold him back. It's his way of doing his bit for the country. You've just gorra let him do what he can.

(**JESSIE** *nods and wipes her eyes.*)

JESSIE. He was right all along you know Mam...about the kids staying in Wales...about them being safe... I only hope he knows how sorry I am...for the things I've said...

MAM. Listen love, we've all said and done things in our lives that we wish we hadn't. I'm the world's worst! Just try not to dwell on it eh?

(*Pause as the bombing intensifies again. As it fades* **JESSIE** *speaks.*)

JESSIE. I wonder how Teresa's getting on? I hope she hasn't gone into labour in the middle of an air raid!

MAM. She'll be fine if she has. They've got great staff on that maternity wing at Mill Road Hospital. You should know – you had your three there.

JESSIE. I'm sure this is the baby's due date.

MAM. Are you sure? ...I'm losing track of the days...

JESSIE. I'm sure it's today. I bumped into Eileen last week and she mentioned today's date. She'll be with her at the birth she said.

MAM. I just hope they're all safe.

JESSIE. Me too. And listen Mam, I don't want you kicking off about where the christening is going to be. We had enough of all that when her and David got married.

MAM. To be honest I'm past caring what religion the baby is Jessie. If there's one good thing that this war has taught me it's that God should protect us all, no matter who we are or what church we worship in.

(*Pause as* **MAM** *clasps her hand in a silent prayer.*)

JESSIE. Mam?

MAM. I'm just praying love... I'm just saying a little prayer for all of us.

> *(The sound of the bombing continues in the darkness. Then the all clear siren finally sounds.)*

> *(**MAM** and **JESSIE** gather their belongings and slowly make their way back home – eventually reaching the Wright household. They drop their belongings in relief.)*

Thank God the house is still standing.

JESSIE. Can't say that for the rest of the street.

MAM. Just count your blessings love.

JESSIE. Did you see the Williamses' house?

MAM. Aye. It's a mess alright.

JESSIE. I'll have to go down later to see if they need a hand with anything. We can always put them up for a few nights if they're struggling.

MAM. Poor beggars.

> *(**MAM** grabs the bedding and blankets they'd taken to the shelter for the night.)*

I'll just take these upstairs.

> *(**MAM** exits. **JESSIE** sits. It's been a long few sleepless nights. She starts to nod off.)*

> *(**PETER**, **EILEEN** and **EDDIE** quietly enter. **EILEEN** is carrying baby Jean swaddled in a shawl.)*

PETER. *(Softly.)* Jessie.

> *(No reply.)*

Jessie love.

*(She jumps up in relief and hugs **PETER**.)*

JESSIE. Peter! Thank God you're safe...

*(**MAM** re-enters room.)*

PETER. Mill Road Infirmary... it's been hit... it's been hit really bad.

JESSIE. Teresa?

MAM. What about Teresa?

*(**EILEEN** starts to softly cry, **EDDIE** comforts her.)*

Oh my God – no...

PETER. It's a miracle this little one's survived.

JESSIE. Poor baby. Poor poor baby.

*(The baby stirs and cries a little. **MAM** steps forward and gently puts her arm around **EILEEN**.)*

MAM. Come on Eileen. Sit down here love. Come on.

EILEEN. I was with her you know, just ten minutes before, on the Maternity Ward with Teresa and the baby. I can't believe it... I just can't believe it.

*(**EILEEN** sheds a tear as **EDDIE** comforts her.)*

EDDIE. No-one can love. But we've got her baby with us still. At least God's spared her little girl.

*(**JESSIE** kneels alongside the baby.)*

JESSIE. She's beautiful... Beautiful.

*(**EILEEN** nods in agreement.)*

EILEEN. *(Panicking a little.)* We'll have to get her baptised as soon as we can won't we Eddie? I don't want anything happening to her if she's not been baptised...

(**EDDIE** *calms her.*)

EDDIE. Don't fret yourself about that love. We'll get it sorted...

EILEEN. At St Alexander's...

(**EILEEN** *looks to* **MAM** *for approval.*)

MAM. You're right Eileen. At St Alexander's, where her mam was married... that's what Teresa would have wanted. And her dad would want that. David would want that too...

(*She gently smiles at* **EDDIE** *and* **EILEEN**. **EILEEN** *responds by holding the baby up to* **MAM**.)

EILEEN. Would you like to hold her Amy? Would you like to hold your granddaughter?

(**MAM** *tenderly takes the baby and cradles her.*)

MAM. Just look at you... Your dad will love you to bits when he comes home. He will you know... and your mam...and our Jean... (*She is near to tears and has to gather herself.*) Your mam...and our Jean...they'll be looking down on you and wishing you all the love and good fortune in the world... They'll be your guardian angels...they will. Your guardian angels...

(**PETER** *takes David's letter from his pocket.*)

PETER. This letter was found tucked in the baby's shawl.

(*Lights dim on the family group who silently gather round* **PETER** *to read the letter as lights come up on* **DAVID** *stood on deck.*)

(**DAVID** *speaks:*)

DAVID. Darling Teresa,

I'm a happy man today. It's been quiet for a little while out here on the ocean waves. I just hope that Liverpool is quiet too, and that you're safe and sound.

I'm really looking forward to getting a telegram soon to say that our baby has finally arrived. Don't forget to give me all the details. Weight, what colour hair, who does the baby look like? You know the sort of thing. I know you've had all the hard work carrying the little one around for nine months, but there's a part of me that would be made up if you write and say the baby is the image of me! I can't help it – you know how vain I am!

I can remember all the excitement when our Peter's kids were born, and how much I used to laugh at him and Jessie being so tired because of all the sleepless nights. But all I do now is look forward to sharing those sleepless nights with you Teresa, and I just can't wait.

I shouldn't really care if we have a boy or a girl, but I'd be chuffed to bits if our first baby is a little girl, and we can have her baptised Jean like we want to. It would mean a lot to me and you, and all of my family.

I can never thank your Aunty Eileen and Uncle Eddie enough for taking good care of you while I'm away. They've been great, and I feel like we're all just part of one big family now.

But my little family, the one I love the most, is you and me – and our baby. You're my wife and my one and only and I miss you and love you SO much. You're going to be a GREAT mum Teresa, and I only wish that I could be there with you as our little one comes into the world.

Let's hope that the war and the waiting will soon be over – and we three can be together and in each other's arms for the rest of our lives.

All my love,

David

(Lights dim on the cast as the image of the radio dominates the stage.)

(It crackles into life.)

RADIO ANNOUNCER. Following the Christmas Blitz in December 1940, Liverpool and Merseyside were constantly bombed for the first eight days of May 1941. Thousands were killed or seriously injured, and tens of thousands were made homeless. In Bootle alone 8,000 homes were destroyed and many more were severely damaged by the incendiary bombs that set the city alight. Much of Liverpool's docklands were crushed by the heavy bombing, and across the River Mersey, Wallasey and the Wirral also suffered terrible losses.

The courage of the civilians who faced death and destruction on the home front should never be forgotten.

Together they overcame a vicious assault on Democracy.

Together they built a new future for their country.

Together they protected the freedom and liberties that we enjoy today.

For others all over the world, the battle for freedom continues.

(The image of the radio fades as lights fade up on the Liverpool scene as before. During the finale song **DAVID**, **TOMMY** *and* **SHIRLEY** *rejoin the family group as though returning at the end of World War Two.)*

(The family group are joined by the **CHORUS** *and* **TERESA** *and* **JEAN** *for the finale as they sing a popular Vera Lynn song from World War Two, a song in the style of "When The*

Lights Go On Again All Over The World".
It should be sung a cappella with a sombre,
slower delivery than the original version.)

(Lights fade on the cast.)

The End

---

* A licence to produce *Waiting* does not include a performance licence for "When The Lights Go On Again All Over The World". The publisher and author suggest that the licensee contact PRS to ascertain the music publisher and contact such music publisher to license or acquire permission for performance of the song. If a licence or permission is unattainable for "When The Lights Go On Again All Over The World", the licensee may not use the song in *Waiting* but should create an original composition in a similar style or use a similar song in the public domain. For further information, please see the Music and Third-Party Materials Use Note on page iii.

www.ingramcontent.com/pod-product-compliance
Lightning Source LLC
La Vergne TN
LVHW051750080426
835511LV00018B/3285